FROM BITTERNESS TO
BETTERNESS

Principles To Change Your Outlook On Life

Mellisha Carter-Linton

Published by

DAYELight
PUBLISHERS

ISBN: 978-1-953759-94-8 (paperback)

Dedication

This book is dedicated to all the young women who had a difficult childhood, suffered emotional pain from bad relationships, and still struggle with emotional scars. Know that you are enough and you are an overcomer. You will get better, overcome life's challenges, and you will walk towards your destiny with God's help.

Dedication

Acknowledgments

I want to thank my Heavenly Father for giving me the wisdom, knowledge, and strength to write this story.

I want to thank my family for their support, especially my children, Adrique and D'Jhanique Linton, and my mother, Luceta Boothe.

Thanks to Andrea Lannaman for inspiring the title and Dionne Taylor for helping me to streamline my thoughts.

A special shout out to Rosemarie Headley, who taught me English Language in High School. God Bless you. Your legacy will live forever.

Table of Contents

Introduction

"It's very important that we own who we are and turn our imperfections into our assets, our vulnerabilities into our strength."

—Diane Von Furstenberg

Relationships are difficult, but they can be even more difficult for a child who lacks the mental and emotional capacity to deal with persons who are deemed to be toxic and have self-esteem issues.

This book "From Bitterness to Betterness" is the story of a young lady named Genie who was born to a teenage mother, who was unprepared for her unwanted arrival. The young mother, though lacking in marketable skills and a proper education, tried her best to provide for them both. Being an underdeveloped child herself, Genie's mom, Mona, did not possess the emotional prowess to deal with being a parent and was also in need of proper parental guidance. Mona's immaturity resulted in her inflicting emotional scars on her young child, and those scars followed her into adulthood.

Genie was exposed to a loveless relationship from an early age by her primary caregiver and she became depressed, miserable, and had constant thoughts of committing suicide. She just wanted to escape the horror and frustration of being an "unwanted child" and always looked down on herself. Genie believed she had no purpose and suffered greatly from low self-esteem, as she was constantly reminded by her mother that she was a mistake, an unwanted pregnancy. This led her to engage in unhealthy relationships with people who meant her no good and did not show her the love and respect she desired and deserved.

The only thing that kept her going was the knowledge of Jesus Christ and her visits to church, where she was taught that Jesus is love and He is a Saviour who gave His life for her. Genie eventually became a parent herself and decided that all the wrongs in her life would not be passed on to her children. She became motivated and driven to succeed and be the best parent for her children. She committed to live a life of forgiveness, continued growth, and purpose with Jesus at the center of all her decisions.

God converted Genie's ashes into beauty, and she now lives like the Queen she was created to be. She did it, and you can too. You have the power to change your story.

Chapter 1

The Struggles Begin

"Every struggle in your life has shaped you into the person you are today. Be thankful for the hard times, they can only make you stronger."

—thedailyquotes.com

This Is How The Story Began

Mona-Lisa Shakespeare grew up in rural Jamaica where the moon-lit skies and stars in their galaxies were the main source of light for the community. The sound of night creatures provided the nightly entertainment along with the telling of duppy stories. Mona-Lisa, like most of the young people in her day, was not exposed to birth control and how to have responsible sexual intercourse. In the 1970s, 1980s, and even 1990s, most parents did not tell their children about the birds and bees, as back then babies came in an airplane, from a pail or a stork, if you reside in North America.

Mona-Lisa lived in the country with a relative. Her mother and father had nine other children at home to take of, and they were doing odd jobs to take care of them. The young child was left alone most of the time to take care of all her domestic needs, parent herself and was not provided with the opportunity to get an education. Mona's mother eventually found a stable job that allowed her to provide for her children. She brought her back to the city, where she was reunited with her other siblings and began her formal education in the primary school system. In the country, a formal education was not seen as important, as farming was the main source of income for most residents and the only purpose of life.

While Mona-Lisa was attending high school, she got pregnant at the age of seventeen for a tall and not very handsome young man named Tom-Strokes Featherweight, who was much older and more experienced than her. At the age of eighteen, this inexperienced Jamaican girl gave birth to a beautiful baby girl who she named Genie Featherweight. After Genie was born, Mona-Lisa was assisted by her parents, but she grew to hate the child because, as far as she was concerned, this child, "the unwanted child," ruined her life but she tried her best to care for the infant. Mona-Lisa, like most teenage mothers, did not plan to be a parent and did not have an adequate formal education. This resulted in her doing odd jobs to support herself and her young child, as the support from her daughter's father, Tom-Strokes, was next to nil. Tom-Strokes, like most men on the island in that

14

era, did not want to live up to his parental responsibilities and questioned the child's paternity.

Tom-Strokes had a rough childhood as his mother died in childbirth and he was raised by his older siblings. His father was there but did not offer much guidance to him, as he worked the farm daily in the cool hills of Manchester to provide for his children. Tom was educationally challenged as children in his era, in the 1950s, were not mandated to attend school as they are now in 21st century Jamaica. He hustled by doing odd jobs to survive. While doing odd jobs he found a mentor who taught him carpentry, which he used to provide for himself.

The Early Struggles

When Genie was six months old, Mona-Lisa lost her mother to cancer, and the stress caused her father to have a stroke, and he too died within six months of his wife's death. Having lost the support of her parents and with older siblings who were not able to assist as they had their own struggles, Mona-Lisa went to live with her child's father, but he was a very abusive young man.

Tom-Strokes lacked the nurturing care of his mother, as he lost her at a tender age. Not experiencing that loving relationship in his early upbringing caused him to lack empathy and made him very inconsiderate. He was just trying to survive. He became an alcoholic, who drank to drown his pain, and when he got drunk, he would inflict blows on Mona-Lisa who would have none of it–she fought hard to defend herself.

He came home late one Friday night expecting a warm meal to be on the table but he did not contribute to the grocery bill, so Mona-Lisa had cooked some porridge from her little hustles. He did not like what he saw and tossed it on her, hurled some insults, and slapped her in the face leaving a scar and swelling. He was very selfish emotionally and financially, always wanting and never quick to give. He gave little or no support to Mona-Lisa or their child. Tom-Strokes gave no support to any of his children and was the first to brag and boast when either of them attained a milestone without his help.

Mona-Lisa and Tom-Strokes continued their abusive relationship, as he got great pleasure from physically abusing women and felt it was his right to discipline them. Genie witnessed the constant physical altercations between her parents and saw the struggles her mother went through so they both could survive. Even though she was about four or five years old, she was very smart. Mona-Lisa washed clothes by hand for other people as a means of providing for her and the infant, as back then people did not have washing machines like they do now on this side of the millennium. Domestic engineering duties such as washing by hand was the main source of income for many women in the late 80s, early 90s, and even today. Mona-Lisa tried her best to take care of little Genie with the funds earned from her odd jobs and eventually built up her nerve and left Mr. Featherweight after years of abuse, which left her body sore and scarred.

The Struggle Continues

"A child that's being abused by their parents does not stop loving their parent, they stop loving themselves." — quotestyle.com

A year or two had passed since Mona-Lisa and Tom-Strokes had been separated, and Mona-Lisa met a much older guy named John Brown. John, for the most part, was a good provider and worked very hard to take care of Mona-Lisa and little Genie, as Tom-Strokes was nowhere in sight and completely reneged all his fatherly duties. They were informed by one of his brothers that he had gone on the farm work program to pick cotton in Canada. Even though John took care of Mona-Lisa and Genie by ensuring they had a roof over their heads and food in their bellies, he too was physically and verbally abusive to Mona-Lisa. She would later marry John, but that did not change how he treated her. Being a young woman with little or no skills, having not finished high school and wanted security for her child, she stayed and took the abuse from John. He accused her constantly of being unfaithful, while at the same time he was eyeing and commingling with every young girl who came in his line of sight.

When Mona-Lisa got frustrated with the treatment being meted out to her by John and remembered that if she did not have Genie to take care of, she would have left long ago, she took out her frustration on the poor child. Genie was called names like "black," "disgusting," and "ugly" and was constantly slapped about most times for doing nothing but breathing. The child was demoralized into thinking she was not worthy of life and love at that young age. The experience gave young Genie a rough physical and emotional start in life. She cried herself to sleep at night, as she could not understand what wrong she had done to be treated so cruelly. The only reason she did not drown in her bed from tears was because it was absorbed by the pillows. She hoped one day that her mother would love her, and she would be treated with tenderness instead of abuse.

We can all relate to Genie's experience as life is like running a race—sometimes there is a false start at the beginning, but we can start afresh. You may not be drowning in tears but self-doubt and low self-esteem, but thank God He is able to give us beauty for our ashes.

Genie found comfort in her favourite words of scripture recorded in 1 Thessalonians 5:16-18 - *"Rejoice always, pray without ceasing, in everything give thanks; for this is the will of God in Christ Jesus for you." (NKJV)*.

You too can find comfort in God's Word.

"Difficult roads lead to beautiful destinations."

—powerfulinsight.com

Chapter 2

The Side Effects Of Being An Unwanted Child

"What is a neglected child? He is a child not planned for, not wanted. Neglect begins, therefore, before he is born."

—Pearl S. Buck

The Abuse Cycle

Mona-Lisa, being a young mother, tried her best to provide for the child even though she still regretted her existence. Genie, only a child, had to endure constant emotional neglect which made her feel so stressed. Her mother never hugged her, never told her positive affirmations like "good job" or "I'm proud of you," and the three words that we all want to hear—I love you—Mona-Lisa never gave them to her yearning child. Every time Genie tried to get a hug from her mom, she was met with blows to the body. At times, Genie just wanted to die; her life felt worthless and useless. Her mother, on the other hand, felt trapped in the abusive relationship but endured it for the sake of Genie, who paid dearly for her mother's decision.

Genie always felt invisible to her mother and was not allowed to voice her feelings because, as far as her mother was concerned, she lacked the mental capacity to understand or hurt emotionally. Mona-Lisa was from the era where children were to be seen and not heard. A child dare not say anything about how they were being treated by their parent or another adult. The words would be punched back down into their throats. They said those were the "good old days." Mona-Lisa's upbringing was not healthy, as it could have been likened to a slave and master relationship.

Toxic And Destructive Emotions

"The true character of a society is revealed in how it treats its children."

—Nelson Mandela

Genie was constantly reminded by her mother that she was a mistake, and the only reason why she existed was because Tom-Strokes had worked voodoo on her (Mona-Lisa). This "voodoo" caused her to feel weak under his charms and resulted in her becoming pregnant. But was it "voodoo," "infatuation," or "love?" Who knows? Mona-Lisa told her daughter how she hated Tom-Strokes and was disgusted whenever she saw him. She had no butterflies in her stomach when she saw him or any intimate feelings for him, but then she found herself helpless in his arms. Not taking responsibility for her actions was a sign of immaturity, as she was in fact still a child.

Mona-Lisa also blamed Genie for the abuse she was receiving from John, as if she was the one inflicting the blows and barking at her. The little girl got so depressed and wondered why she was born, why her mother did not give her to the State or give her up for adoption to a suitable family, since she never wanted her. Genie became an introvert, and she thought of running away several times but there was nowhere to go. She continued crying herself to sleep at night—which became her hobby—after being overwhelmed with blame for adult decisions and actions. She prayed that God would come or send an angel or someone to rescue her. No one came.

As time progressed, Genie suffered psychologically while Mona-Lisa suffered physically and mentally at the hands and descriptive words from John. Genie felt so unloved at home, so after school she would stay on the streets loitering until she got tired enough and then went home. She was afraid to go to the house because it was not a home but a constant battlefield and a place of dejection. The house could have been likened to the judgment that Jesus spoke of in Mark 9:48 where it was stated that hell would be a place *"where their worm does not die and the fire is not quenched."* (NKJV). Genie lived in constant torment.

23

Genie endured constant rejection from a parent she looked up to and someone who should have been her closest ally; this made Genie emotionally weak, angry, and a suicidal teenager with low self-esteem. She was made to believe that she was to be treated poorly and be the door mat of other people. During those tumultuous years of growing up, the only ray of hope for Genie was her trips to Sunday School, where she learnt about God and real love.

She began to read her Bible to know more about this Jesus and His plans for her life and was intrigued by John 3:16 where it states that *"For God so loved the world that he gave His holy begotten Son, that whoever believes in Him should not perish but have everlasting life."* (NKJV). This made her feel special. Faith in Jesus made Genie a focused young girl and helped her as she transitioned to a young lady. Being a follower of Jesus Christ helped her through the difficult teenage years when the hormones were raging, knowing that any sexual contact with someone of the opposite sex is a sin (fornication). She worked very hard to follow the will of Jesus Christ even without the support of her parent, but the Lord provided people to help her on the journey of life.

As the years rolled over, John Brown died as he was a substance abuser. It seems like Genie's mom was attracted to a certain type of man. Mona-Lisa and Genie were alone again, but instead of bonding through a difficult financial and emotional storm, Genie was still treated like her mother's stepchild.

24

Plans To Self-Destruct

Genie worked very hard at being a successful woman and building on the educational foundation given to her by John Brown, but she still struggled. When she was in her early twenties, she sought out members of the opposite sex in an attempt to find a good heterosexual relationship, but the quality of men she encountered was extremely poor. She had terrible experiences, and the kind of males she attracted were either not very ambitious, liars, or in relationships. She formed a negative impression of the male gender, as all the men she encountered just wanted to use and abuse her. Genie was trying to find that love and sense of belonging that she never had growing up, but she was attracting the males that represented how she felt about herself.

Genie always felt unwanted and unloved, and the thought of ending it all by suicide crossed her mind several times. There was one time in particular when she was so overwhelmed and planned to put an end to the emotional pain she endured in the past and continued to experience by walking into oncoming traffic on a busy thoroughfare in the city. After all, she was unwanted and would not have been missed, especially by her mother. Mona-Lisa would surely like that as she would be finally free of the chains that shackled her for most of her life.

As Genie stood staring mindlessly at the fast-driving vehicles, her body was crippled. Her legs remained planted, and sheer heaviness overcame her body. At that moment, a gentle thought floated through her mind. She remembered the words of scripture she always read in Jeremiah 29:11 *"For I know the plans I have for you, "declares the Lord," plans to prosper you and not to harm you, plans to give you hope and a future." (NIV)*. At that moment, it brought life to her, and she made a new choice. Genie immediately pulled back and walked away. "God is my strength. In Him will I trust," she breathed the words slowly, and an air of relief overcame her as she felt the presence of the Holy Spirit.

"Children are human beings to whom respect is due, superior to us by reason of the innocence and of the greater possibilities of their future."

—Maria Montessori

Chapter 3

Power To Forgive

"To forgive is to set a prisoner free and discover that the prisoner was you."

—Lewis B. Smedes

The Toxic Results

Genie was rejected before she was born, and this caused her to endure immeasurable psychological stress that made her emotionally hard, angry and apprehensive. Despite her rough early life experiences, she still desired to find love and lead a normal life.

The need to be loved and appreciated caused her to lower/compromise her standards, morals, values, and Christian beliefs, which resulted in her making poor relationship choices. The negative experiences she had growing up, of being rejected, unloved, and being constantly reminded that she was a mistake, led her to believe that was how she was to be treated, as though she had no worth or purpose on the earth. This resulted in her attracting undesirable males into her life, and she just felt like a broken vessel leaking out its precious contents.

She Met A Conman

When Genie was twenty-five, she met a young man who was two years her senior through a mutual friend, Paul Thompson, who she knew from her teenage years. Paul was a good marketer; he should have opened a dating business. He told Genie how his friend, Bobby Chunks, was a hard-working young man, and he would be a wonderful husband. Paul brought Bobby to meet Genie, who she thought wasn't really her type at first, and it took some warming up to him. After all, she was still dealing with her scars being in close contact with her mom.

Bobby was a persistent young man who pursued Genie tirelessly as if he was desperate for her love. Due to her dysfunctional past, she did not know that this could have possibly been a red flag about Bobby, as she was desperate for the attention she was getting. I guess his efforts paid off as within a couple of months of them courting, they were walking down the aisle. He was just an evil manipulator who preyed on Genie's low self-esteem. He was an emotional abuser, neglectful, and a toxic person and he found an easy target.

The Marriage From Hell

"Be careful with who you start dating. A lot of people aren't looking for love, they're looking for help."

—Stephan Labossiere

Genie and Bobby quickly began to work on expanding their family, and within the first five years they had three children: twin boys and a girl. Even though she still struggled with her emotional scars from her childhood, Genie worked hard to provide for her family which kept her focused on achieving her goals and making a better life. She was optimistic about her marriage and family and looked to a successful future, but Bobby Chunks had other plans. Bobby too came with his childhood emotional baggage which made him into an ace emotional abuser. He used the low self-esteem issues of Genie to his advantage to manipulate her into marrying him, claiming that he loved her. The truth was, he and his friend Paul developed a plan for him to move out of his less than favourable living conditions that he shared with several siblings, parents, and other relatives. Genie was unknowingly a pawn in this evil plot to help him out of his quagmire.

She was employed to a good company in the medical supplies industry and was on the verge of being promoted to supervisor. The new position had growth potential for future promotions to management. This gave Bobby Chunks some status, as her salary could afford him the high lifestyle he

29

wanted, and soon they purchased a house in one of those high-end gated communities with a swimming pool. He attached himself like a leech to suck her dry, while she thought she was a member of a formidable team.

Bobby's Story

Bobby's father, Freddy Chunks, physically and emotionally abused his mother, Mary Chunks, young Bobby, and his other siblings. Freddy was also unfaithful to Miss Mary and had some outside children. Miss Mary stayed in the abusive relationship, and her children witnessed all the blows she got and all the unfaithfulness she endured, as she did nothing to change her situation. Bobby Chunks thought that was the way relationships were supposed to be; hence, he turned out just like his father and expected his wife to be just like his mother; staying at home washing, cooking, and cleaning while he goes out and enjoy himself with his lovers and male friends.

The Struggle Persists

"Don't settle for almost good enough. Go get what you deserve, even if it's harder to find."

—Stephan Labossiere

Living with Bobby was extremely difficult for Genie as his intentions were not about love and care but to manipulate. This made him emotionally unavailable and disabled him in giving Genie the love and respect she wanted. He was insecure and was always seeking the approval of others. He also displayed insecurity in their relationship, irrespective of the fact that they were together for many years. Bobby's attitude most times made him intolerable and resulted in an emotional wedge and lack of intimacy between him and Genie. He had a problem with everything she did. He complained constantly while doing nothing to help with family demands like paying the bills or spending time with the family. It was pure misery whenever he was around.

Genie was annoyed by his attitude and wondered what she had gotten herself into. This man was similar to her father and the man her mother married. She was distressed. She thought about getting a divorce several times due to his unbearable attitude and unfaithfulness. How much can one person really take before blowing a fuse!

Bobby's Betrayal

"There are always people willing to commit unspeakable human atrocity in exchange for a little power and privilege."
—Chris Hedges

Bobby Chunks had a thing for getting involved with his female coworkers and enjoyed having extra-marital affairs. He was the consummate adulterer. He was neglectful to his family and spent most of his money and time impressing his friends and scouting out new prospects, while his wife had to resort to begging from her family and friends to feed the children and send them to school.

After ten years of marriage, Genie finally got the willpower to leave Bobby Chunks. As Genie planned on seeking legal counsel, she had to have an emergency surgery as her appendix had ruptured. She had to rely on close friends and the children's grandparents to assist as Bobby was nowhere to be found. When Genie had recovered from this near-fatal life-changing experience, she retained legal counsel to start the divorce proceedings. The absence of Bobby during that critical period was the straw that broke the camel's back.

As expected, when the family needed him the most, Bobby was up to no good. One of Genie's friends saw him on the north coast while she was in the hospital. He was seen with what appeared to be a pregnant woman. Genie contacted the Eagle's Private Eye Consultants Ltd. and did some private investigative work on Bobby and found that he got one of his coworkers pregnant. Soon after Bobby's return, he started arguing with Genie for her to leave the dwelling. He and his new love devised a plan to get rid of Genie by changing the locks on the house, so he could get the house that he and his wife bought for this new baby mother. He was very ruthless, as he was willing to put his current children out in the cold for this new person. What kind of monster would evict his children for a woman? Bobby Chunks.

How Did Delilah Come Into The Picture?

Since no one wanted to see Bobby at home because of the mayhem that occurred with his constant complaints and quarrels about petty things, he spent most of his time claiming to be at work. This gave him an opportunity to scout out new prospects such as Delilah Iscariot, who he could manipulate and tell how worthless his wife was and how she did not take care of him, when all he did was cause problems and embarrassment with the neighbours from his loud quarrels. Bobby and Delilah spent quality time together at the expense of his family who hardly saw him. She told him all the things he wanted to hear and was clingy and needy unlike Genie who, though scarred, was somewhat independent being an only child. They were at a resort on the north coast when Genie required emergency surgery. He had packed his bag and left the family home earlier in the week, again claiming to be at work out of town.

Retribution

As it turns out, the new lady (Delilah Iscariot) was exactly what the doctor ordered for Bobby. She made sure he did for her all he never did for Genie and their children and had him taking care of her son, mother, dog, and cat. They had their bundle of joy on the way, and they were over the moon about starting their new life together.

Bobby was so love-struck or dumbstruck that he did not even realize he was being used the same way he used Genie to get ahead in life. The baby was born within six months of him evicting Genie and her children from the family home, and now Delilah was the new woman of the house. He soon realized the kind of woman Delilah was. One day he came home from work and found another male with his new love in a compromising position, which is only fair since he did the same thing to Genie when they were married. They say revenge is a dish best served cold, but this revenge was not being served by Genie but the laws of life and nature. Genie was very angry about being thrown out of the house she helped to purchase and now had to be living with relatives, but she decided to leave everything in God's capable hands. She reminded herself of the words of scripture recorded in Romans 12:19, where it states *"Don't try to get revenge for yourselves, my dear friends, but leave room for God's wrath. It is written, Revenge belongs to me; I will pay it back, says the Lord."* (CEB).

Healing And Forgiveness

"Don't regret being a good woman to the wrong man; it's his loss."

—**Stephan Labossiere**

Even though Genie had a rough childhood and experienced a failed marriage despite her best efforts at communication and restoration, she still got up each day to face life as she had the power of the Holy Spirit and the desire to provide for her children. Her heart was still broken from the betrayal of Bobby and how he went about discarding her and the children, which left her feeling like she was literally stabbed in the back. She thought they were a team, building a family, only to find out that Bobby was building a future at his family's expense with another person. Genie also had to deal with her mother, who offered her no support emotionally, as she was a gossiper and all of her daughter's struggle was the hot topic of her days, weeks, months, and year. She had to turn to the one person who could mend her heart and give her the strength to go on, and that was the Holy Spirit. After a few months of fasting and praying, she was fully recovered from the surgery and her emotional injuries, and she was energised and ready to take on the world.

Genie rented a house as her life improved and took up gardening, which helped her to find peace and relax her mind. She also began journaling her days and also spent a lot of time in the Word of God as she embarked on a journey of forgiving Bobby and her parents. She also joined a gym to work on her physical body, as after years of taking care of family and home, she had neglected to take care of herself. After watching several hours of Joel Osteen's sermons and reading lots of empowerment literature online, she decided that she was no longer going to be a victim but a victor. She was going to dig herself further out of the pit by being a mentor to young ladies through the company Foundation that adopted a centre for at-risk girls.

She focused on self-improvement and decided the struggles she endured as a child, wife, and mother would not be reflected in how she treated her children or others. Genie taught her children about Jesus and His saving grace, and she reassured them that they are important, they have the capacity to change the world, and there is greatness within them.

Genie decided that she was going to take control of her life, forgive, rise above her childhood trauma and failed marriage, and began working on a bright and prosperous future for herself and her children.

How Unforgiveness Affected Genie

Genie suffered great emotional abuse from she was a child. She was deeply scarred and suffered from self-doubt, even thought she had to be perfect to fit in and always gave 110% to her tasks and family to feel loved and accepted, but that was still not good enough. She became bitter from the betrayal of Bobby, the insults, bad treatment, and lack of support from her mother (nothing had changed besides the years) and was a miserable individual to be around. She was always snapping at the children like a snapping turtle and developed an irregular heartbeat and a slightly elevated blood pressure.

She soon realised that the unforgiveness she held on to was the source of her stress. The records of past hurt that she kept playing in her head, the victim stamp that she wore on her forehead and in her eyes, and the unprocessed emotions from childhood, caused her to be angry and unbearable to be around. The unforgiveness was affecting her health, relationship with the children, and performance at work. She had a light-bulb moment when she realised how heavy laden she felt, like a donkey carrying hampers on both sides, how tired, stressed, and exhausted she felt, and she also had headaches daily. She decided at that moment that she would forgive all the persons who had done her wrong, as she was the person that was being affected as the toxic culprits were out and about enjoying their lives.

Peace And Fulfilment

Genie's life became fulfilling when she let go of the heavy load of unforgiveness. She decided that she was not going to wait around for the people who hurt her to make an apology, especially if the person thought they did nothing wrong and are in fact (in their mind) the real victim in the situation. Even though she did not condone or approve of her abusers' actions, she decided it was more important to set herself free from the bondage of her scars, enjoy the blessings of God and her children and look forward to living a peaceful life. She decided that the sharks (unforgiveness and bitterness) of her life won't eat her alive, as she was going to forgive and thrive.

Forgiving and releasing the unprepared parents who tried their best under the circumstances allowed Genie to have a different perspective on life and their decisions. Even though she suffered immensely, she used the lemons and made lemonade.

Genie decided that she was going to love herself and others and that she was no longer going to miss out on the beauty that life had to offer by labeling herself as a victim. She already had high blood pressure and heart problems from her ordeals, and she was not going to risk having a heart attack or stroke, leaving her children motherless. The joy of the Lord was better.

"The weak can never forgive. Forgiveness is the attribute of the strong."

—Mahatma Gandhi

Chapter 4

Beauty For Ashes

"There are two kinds of pain: the pain of change and the pain of never changing and remaining the same."

—*Joyce Meyer, Beauty for Ashes: Receiving Emotional Healing*

Life Happens To Us All

"Easy is not an option. No days off. Never quit. Be fearless. Talent you have naturally. Skill is only developed by hours and hours of work."

—Usain Bolt

Genie's life was a series of challenges and had more valley than mountain top experiences. She felt like Job from the Bible most of her days because of the continuous calamities that she had to go through and thought that probably she should have entered the Olympics or world champions hurdling races. During those difficult days, she spent more time with Jesus and saw improvements in their relationship. At the end of each episode, she was more focused, garnered more wisdom, learnt a new skill, got a new certification, spent more time in prayer, and got her fight back and soul restored.

Choosing To Find Beauty

After Genie Featherweight endured years of emotional abuse from her primary caregiver, and both emotional and financial abuse from her former husband, she dug deep and found her inner strength and relied heavily on her faith in God. She began to seek the Lord for the lessons to be learnt from her life experiences and the way forward.

Even though she hurt greatly, Genie was in a better position to understand the struggles of the girls she mentored with the Foundation, as she empathized with them. While her mother was mistreating her, she knew how that pain felt, and she knew how not to treat people and how to speak to persons to build their self-esteem instead of finding words to tear them down. She learnt how to be a better parent and the type of emotional support that children require, so they can be well-rounded and emotionally healthy individuals.

Since her former husband was never around, she learnt a lot of property management skills such as minor plumbing and carpentry. She became an excellent landscaper and understood some aspects of construction. Genie's self-confidence and independence grew because she had to do so much for herself and the children financially and otherwise.

Bobby thought that when he left her alone, she would have been crying and falling apart, waiting for him to come and save her so he could feel superior. Genie refused to be placed in a box by people who meant her no good. She relied heavily on her faith and kept on encouraging herself in the Lord.

Being a mother is a great responsibility, a blessing, and a privilege that Genie did not take lightly. There are so many females who are unable to bear a child. Being chosen for the awesome role of being a parent got Genie fired up about the future. She wanted to ensure that the next generation had better life experiences than she did. To achieve this milestone, Genie ensured that her children never missed school. They were well educated both in the formal education system and about the Kingdom of the living God and the importance of including Him in all their decisions. She offered them guidance daily in coping with difficult situations that they encountered and tried her very best to explain the emotional effects of their experiences, especially in coping with toxic persons like their father and grandmother. She wanted to ensure that the actions she took when faced with life's challenges communicated the right message to her children, as these lessons would affect how they made decisions when they became adults. Genie did not want them to end up like their father, Bobby Chunks, who displayed poor decision-making and had a rotten behaviour. Genie made it a point of duty to always learn something new, whether formally or informally, so the children would see and understand that nothing in this life is unachievable, and we must never stop in the storm like the ones she endured.

The Makings Of Beauty From Ashes

"The struggle of life is one of our greatest blessings. It makes us patient, sensitive and God-like. It teaches us that although the world is full of suffering, it is also full of overcoming of it."

—Helen Keller

When the struggles got too much for Genie, she found her strength and peace in the Word and giving praise to God. She knew that giving up was not an option, as there were people's destinies that were tied to her succeeding and fulfilling her destiny, as the Israelites needed Moses to help them out of Egypt to the promised land of Canaan. She did not let her limitations of being an introvert and lack of knowledge in some areas stop her from achieving her goals. She was confident that God would send help when the situation required it, or He would give her the strength required.

Genie decided to use the example of King Solomon and constantly prayed and asked the Lord for wisdom and the spirit of discernment to see the beauty of all her ashes experiences. She remained in tune with the Holy Spirit and found that she was more efficient and effective in performing her duties, and she was finding lessons or gems from her life challenges. Genie's spiritual muscle became stronger; she became more confident after spending a lot of time in the Word. She found it easier to tell others about Christ, how good He was and how relevant He was in her life. She stopped dropping her anchor when the storms of life racked her ship but rode out the storm as they came up.

Despite all the difficulties faced by Genie, she still pressed forward, realizing that she was still standing having survived a horrible childhood, tumultuous teenage years, a near fatal medical incident, and being married to an evil deceiver. She decided that her children would come out without the smell of smoke as the three Hebrew boys, Shadrach, Meshach and Abednego. She channeled her negative experiences, failures, and heartaches into life goals. She went on to enroll in a local university to pursue her master's degree, as she was placed in an acting manager position at work but would be confirmed in the post when she had the requisite qualifications.

Create A Vision For The Future And Executing

Many are the afflictions of the righteous, and Genie knows firsthand what this means. Despite trying to live a life of integrity, her mother thought she was not a good daughter because she was not taking all her salary to her when she worked. While her husband thought she was not a good wife because she did not sit around and take his abuse, disrespect, and womanizing. Judas taught her that betrayal and backstabbing always occur in the inner circle, as the enemies on the outside can't get close enough to know your business and hurt you. Being an only child, Genie had many sessions of self-talk with herself, of course, not speaking out loud. She assessed her status and asked herself some tough questions, such as: What legacy do I want to leave for my children? What should my life look like in ten years? What am I passionate about? What does life success look like to me? How much is all this dreaming and planning going to cost, and how is it going to be financed? What do I want to be remembered for when I have crossed over into the sweet by and by?

Terri Savelle Foy, in her book "Dream it. Pin it. Live it. Make Vision Boards Work For You," highlighted the importance of having a vision board and its significance in personal development. Habakkuk 2:2-3 reads, *"And the LORD answered me, and said, Write the vision, and make it plain upon tables, that he may run that readeth it. For the vision is yet for an appointed time, but at the end it shall speak and not lie: though it tarry, wait for it; because it will surely come, it will not tarry."* (KJV). Genie made a vision board, and one of her plans was to open her own business.

Being in close association with the Foundation at her workplace, she felt the need to further help the young women in the program, and with her years of leadership experience, she decided to open a small sewing company. The young ladies who participated in the Foundation Program received training in sewing, baking, interior design, among other things. Genie soon realized that even though the ladies were fully certified and well skilled, most of them were not utilizing their new skills and decided to find a solution to help them. Genie's Design Limited was launched within a month of her promotion at her substantive job, and she was able to employ three ladies from the program at the opening of business, which saw a steady increase in customers and revenue. She could see a change in the lives of the young ladies who began to earn their independence and also pursued further studies. Some sought other employment, which created an opportunity for young talent to join. A few original employees remained to train and guide the new staff because they were loyal to Genie.

In reflecting, Genie saw how God used her struggles to change the life of herself and her children for the better and also the lives of several young ladies, who would have been lost in the system and may have become teenage mothers themselves. Genie was now a successful businesswoman with multiple streams of income. Her ashes was turned to beauty because God intervened, and she refused to drop her anchor in the storm.

Mellisha Carter-Linton

"No matter what happens to us, we must have no time for regrets. Life is all about movement. We Learn, We Grow, We Move."

—MordyQuotes

Chapter 5

Pursue Your Purpose

"Believe you can and you're halfway there."

—Theodore Roosevelt

God's Purpose Is Unstoppable

"Jealousy is a good indication that you are doing things the right way. People never get jealous of losers."

—mediawebapps.com

In Genesis 37, the story is told of Jacob who had twelve sons but he loved Joseph more because he was the son of his old age. Jacob made his special son a tunic of many colours to the envy of his brothers. They hated Joseph because he was a dreamer and told them that they would bow down and worship him, as he had seen in his dream. He was not thinking anything about what he dreamt but just imagine how the blood in his brothers' bodies was boiling when they heard him say these things. These brothers would later conspire to kill Joseph but decided to sell him into slavery

47

to a caravan of Ishmaelites heading to Egypt, where he would later fulfil his purpose.

Genie knew exactly how Joseph felt being rejected, cast down, and being buried alive by the hate of other persons because they thought he was a threat to their existence. Genie was not only treated poorly by her mother and husband but there were two co-workers who conspired to make her very uncomfortable at work. They told lies to the manager about her slacking off on her duties while they were the lazy ones, and they did not like the change in status quo that she brought with her hard-working can-do attitude. She was very ambitious and that was an issue. They were comfortable doing the little work for the little pay and had no plans of sinking their safe ship. One of her co-workers was even upset that after getting a promotion to supervisor, he was required to do more work and blamed her for him taking on a promotion that he did not plan to work in. Genie had a strong work ethic and was dedicated; she soon left those laggards behind.

Throughout Genie's life, she encountered people that were time wasters, believed in handouts, blamed people for their life failures, and were jealous of her and her achievements. She did nothing special as everyone gets the same 24 hours each day to make something of themselves. What she found was that people were lazy and were satisfied with living a mediocre life, but she did not believe in burying her talents but decided to live a life emptied out to fulfil God's purpose.

Proverbs 24:30-31 states that *"I went to the field of the lazy man, And by the vineyard of the man devoid of understanding; And there it was, all overgrown with thorns; Its surface was covered with nettles; Its stone wall was broken down."* (NJKV). Verses 33-34 states *"A little sleep, a little slumber, A little folding of the hands to rest; So shall your poverty come like a prowler, And your need like an armed man."* (NKJV). Genie wanted to prosper, as being attacked by poverty seemed more terrifying that being successful. So she decided to capitalise on every opportunity presented to her, to use her talents to make a difference in the lives of her family and persons she encountered.

Genie always had a desire to learn new skills and unearth her talents, so instead of internalising the pain of being neglected by her husband, she went and learnt how to design drapery and learnt interior decorating rather than sitting around in self-pity. This exposure gave her the knowledge she needed and desire to open her own business, along with the need to build up other females. She empathised with broken people, especially females, and she believed strongly in upskilling herself and empowering others through mentoring.

The negative life experiences endured by Genie were designed by the enemy to destroy her so she would not use the talents that the Lord had blessed her with to make a difference in her generation. Instead of breaking her down, the struggles actually built her up; she conquered her Goliaths and ascended to her throne like King David.

When the days got tough, she reminded herself that she was a child of God, a child of purpose and a mighty warrior like Gideon, and all things were working together for her good.

What Is Your Purpose?

"The two most important days in life are the day you were born and the day you find out why."

—Mark Twain

When Genie was a little girl and used to cry herself to sleep at night, she wondered why she was born to suffer being constantly abused and humiliated by her parent. How could a God of love put a child in such a hostile, hateful environment? If every child was born with a purpose, what was hers? Jesus came to save humanity from their sin and eternal damnation; Moses came to save the Israelites from Pharaoh, and Steve Jobs created Apple. She prayed and asked the Lord to reveal His will to her and reminded herself of Psalms 139:15-16, "*My frame was not hidden from you when I was made in the secret place, when I was woven together in the depths of the earth. Your eyes saw my unformed body; all the days ordained for me were written in your book before one of them came to be.*" (NIV).

Genie did not know what her purpose was, but she felt deep within that there was something that the Lord wanted her to do. She had dreams of one day owning her own business, but when she told her husband or other close family members, they would let her know that she did not have what it takes to be a business owner. Some wanted her to play it safe and just do the regular 9 to 5 job like everybody else because that income was secure. Like Joseph dreamt that people would have been bowing down to him and it materialized, she believed that her dreams too would come to pass. She found that her family members may have had good intentions in not wanting her to take the risk of venturing into the business world, but she was the one who had the dream, and her destiny was dependent on it.

Pursuing Purpose Despite The Obstacles

"It always seems impossible until it's done."
—Nelson Mandela

Genie knew all too well about being told what she is not or what she would never be and being constantly put down or placed in a box, so other people could feel superior or accomplished. Could it be that these hard life lessons learnt by Genie would allow her to help other broken people and empathize with those who were treated as outcasts?

When she was a child, she maintained her sanity and some amount of self-worth and direction through her relationship

51

with Jesus Christ. She read His Word, believing that she was created for a greater good. Being a mother herself, she ensured that her children and young people with whom she associated knew their worth, and she offered encouragement and guidance when the opportunity presented itself. Genie loved Jesus from she was a little girl, and when she would tell people that she was a Christian, she was called a "grease can" and told that she was not good enough to be aligned with Jesus.

For someone who struggled with being accepted for most of her life, being told that she was a "grease can" caused her to question whether Jesus could really love an unlovable, unwanted child like her. She would often fall back into the pit of despair. She wasn't aware that the enemy could send people as distractions to take her off the course that Jesus planned for her before she was even born.

Despite the lack of support from family members and close friends, Genie decided that she was going to succeed. She would use each brick thrown at her as a stepping stone as there is normally victory on the other side of struggles. She just continued praying and reminded herself of Psalms 30:5 *"...Weeping may endure for a night, But joy comes in the morning."* (NKJV). When she got really low and tired both mentally and physically, she reminded herself that she was in the fight of her life. She was in the water being chased by sharks, and if she stopped, she would be devoured by the sharks of anger, bitterness, and frustration as she tried to wait patiently for God to answer her prayers.

Unleashing The Pearls

"An arrow can only be shot by pulling it backward. When life is dragging you back with difficulties, it means it's going to launch you into something great. So just focus and keep going."

—Educated Finds/Facebook [educatedbox.com]

Life pulled Genie back when she had to undergo emergency surgery and when she was betrayed by her husband. Life was always pulling her back with one crisis after another, and she had to be constantly defending herself and clawing back into life, grasping it with both hands, like a rock climber on the ledge of a mountain. She wished her life was different and she would get some rest from the constant struggles of self-doubt and constant conflicts in defending herself. She learnt that the struggles made her stronger mentally, stronger spiritually, as she spent more time on her knees praying and seeking wisdom from God. The process and all her experiences were unleashing the pearls in her, as she put away insecurity, suicidal thoughts, lack of purpose and direction, neglect from parents and spouse, and became empowered and strong. She began to impact lives through her mentorship work and also the lives of many females who were touched by working at her company. She was now somebody of value, and the crushing squeezed the pearls out of her and made her a very kind and supportive woman.

"If you want to achieve your goals, help others achieve their goals."

—**Zig Ziglar**

Chapter 6

Break Generational Curse

"Hurt people, hurt people. That's how pain patterns get passed on, generation after generation after generation. Break the chain today. Meet anger with sympathy, contempt with compassion, and cruelty with kindness. Greet grimaces with smiles. Forgive and forget about finding fault. Love is the weapon of the future."

—Yehuba Berg

What Is A Generational Curse?

According to the Gospel Coalition, a "generational curse describes the cumulative effect on a person of things that their ancestors did, believed or practiced in the past and a consequence of an ancestor's actions, beliefs and sins being passed down." [The Source.org]

Genie was the victim of a generational curse, as all her mother's bitterness, resentment, life insecurities, and

55

mediocre thinking were passed down to her. For a long time, she lived in fear of what people thought because that was how her mother taught her; that people's opinions about her life were more important than what she thought about herself. She was taught life was just about getting by and not stepping out of the boat like Peter in faith, trying new things, seeing new people and places. The curses that she was under made her think that she had to be dependent on a spouse or some other thing to have an identity for herself. She was not taught that she was royalty and a child of the Most High God.

Generational Blessings

In the Book of Genesis, the Lord told Father Abraham that he would be a father of many nations. Jesus is a descendant of Abraham, who came to bless us by dying for our sins. Jesus came to change the status quo and break tradition, and Genie decided that she was going to do the same. She made up her mind that her children were going to be different. They were not going to be mediocre in thinking or living as she was when she was growing up. She ensured they got the love and attention they should even though she did not have a good relationship with their father. Unlike her mother, Mona-Lisa, she was not going to let her children believe that her life challenges was their fault. She was accountable and took responsibility for her own actions, and made sure that their environment was comfortable and filled with love which allowed them to strive and grow into healthy individuals.

Generational blessings or curses are very important and cannot be taken for granted because they have the potential to shift the future of a generation or a nation for better or worst.

Parents, Be Careful

Bobby Chunks was an adult in this right mind, and he had the authority to break the generational curse from his father over his life. He chose to be like his father, not respecting or valuing women and pretending that he loved them so he could manipulate them. He felt superior to them when he had more money than them and was in control of their purse strings, so to speak. Bobby decided to use his experiences to hurt other people so others would be dysfunctional like he was. He constantly played mind games and gaslighted Genie when they were married.

He was the first to tell people how he was a good provider and father to their children, while Genie was a no-good wife. What kind of person in their right mind would waste their time honouring a man who prefers to spend all his time and money with his friends, while neglecting his wife and children? He was not worthy of honour partly because he was never around to be a part of their lives and expected things to get done, and somehow family expenses and chores were that of his wife and not his. Bobby constantly complained when he was asked to make a simple contribution to a home enhancement project or a family event, but he had no problem paying for all-inclusive weekends for his friends. What lessons was he teaching his children? That strangers are more important than them.

Change The Script

"Children have never been very good at listening to their elders but they have never failed to imitate them."

—James Baldwin

Genie was a smart woman, and she learnt some lessons along the way about the beauty of serving God. What is hidden from others is always revealed to the children of God. While Bobby was having a blast with his friends, Genie was planning and strategizing the lives of herself and their children. Genie made up her mind that she was not going to be like Mary Chunks, who sat down in a dysfunctional relationship just to wear a ring. Genie could afford to visit the jewelry store and purchase her own ring if she wanted to wear a ring. She decided that her children would see a better example of someone knowing their worth.

She knew that as a parent, her actions would have more of an impact on her children than what she said, and decided that she was going to live out the Christ example for them to follow. Genie wanted her children to know that it was okay to walk away from toxic people and situations to protect their sanity and self-image.

Genie wanted her sons to know that women were to be respected and treated like Queens, that they are individuals who can make their own decisions, quite capable of being independent, and, in fact, a good woman is a prize. She is to be treated like an equal partner, with whom life decisions would be made, and if they were so blessed to be chosen by a female to be a husband, that they should work together with Jesus to build their relationship and family.

Genie wanted her daughter to know that as a female and an individual, she was created by God with value, dreams, and purpose and was not a second-rate citizen or a person of no significance. She was to be nobody's floor mat, and if she encountered a relationship of any kind where she felt she was not being valued, it was time to take up herself and leave. Genie wanted her to be independent and not dependent on anyone to make life decisions for her, to continually educate herself, and always strive to be independent and strong-willed.

Breaking The Curse

Genie knew that she was created by God as a unique individual and was fully equipped to make her own decisions and strive on her own. She decided that she was not going to self-destruct but use the lessons learnt to drive her ambition and purpose and that she was going to be a successful parent and woman. She knew that, like a seed planted in the right environment, she had to change her environment to create a positive atmosphere for herself and the children. From the day she was born, she was surrounded by negativity. She was constantly told by her parent that she was unwanted and a mistake, and she faced physical and emotional abuse from a parent that was frustrated by her existence. Her situation was further exacerbated when she married a con man who abused her emotionally and financially. Genie wanted a fresh start, so she sold her business to one of her employees and migrated to Canada to start a new life in a new country with more opportunities for herself and her children.

Change Your Environment And Change Your Life

"When you cut off someone from your life, they will never tell people the full story. They will only tell them the part that makes you look bad and them innocent."

—Word Porn

Bobby Chunks was living in the house that Genie was still paying for, and he was still talking bad about her, claiming that she was a bad parent and was not making her equal contribution to financing the children. He claimed that she was a negative influence on the children, which was a rather strange thing for him to say considering he hardly spent time with his family. He also still wanted her to contribute more to the children's maintenance, even though she was basically paying his mortgage, until the legal process of asset separation was finalised.

Bobby launched a full marketing campaign against Genie, telling lies to whoever would listen to him, trying to ruin her character, and painted himself as the victim of a horrible wife. He told lies, saying she was unfaithful to him with multiple partners and questioned the paternity of the children and lamented how financially distressed he was from being the only one who took care of the family expenses. The truth was that he was taking care of a family, just not his. He told her that no one would want her with all those children and also because of her age. Just as Jesus was wrongfully accused and was led away as a lamb to be slaughter, Genie remained silent. This was one of the motivating factors that caused Genie to take the children to live in Canada to free them from the negativity and hostility.

"The less you respond to negative people, the more peaceful your life will become."

—**www.itsalovelylife.com**

Chapter 7

Create Your Future Road Map

"Planning is bringing the future into the present so that you can do something about it now."

—Alan Lakein

Chart Your Course

Genie believed in setting goals, and this was reaffirmed when she read Proverbs 29:18 which states that *"Where there is no vision, the people perish: but he that keepeth the law, happy is he."* (KJV). She knew the goals that she had achieved was because she had made a map (vision board) of where she wanted to be in the future, and she would have been a failure without her activity planner. She also learnt that the setting of goals was from the beginning of time, as the Creator of the Universe laboured for six days preparing the earth for humanity so we would have everything to our comfort on earth. Genie believed that God still planned for her, as she awoke each day to fulfil His purpose and was encouraged by Jeremiah

29:11 which states, *"For I know the thoughts that I think toward you, says the Lord, thoughts of peace and not of evil, to give you a future and a hope."* (NKJV). She continued to seek God's face for His help and wisdom.

Achieving Purpose

Genie felt that she was created for a purpose and she was brought back from that near-death experience of a ruptured appendix to make the world a better place. Genie had a challenging childhood, but she decided that she was going to make something of herself and change her story. She achieved her personal targets by taking a few systematic steps to reach her goals, but what is a goal? A goal is the end towards which effort is directed, according to the Merriam Webster dictionary. The experts tell us that goals must be SMART and must include the following steps:

Specific

There must be some specific things you want to achieve. You can start the process by making a vision board as mentioned in Chapter 4. As a goal setter, you are encouraged to write down your plans in a sentence that encapsulates your goals in very specific terms.

Measurable

In making the strategic plan for the achievement of your goals, performance standards must be established to facilitate measurement. This allows you to determine

64

whether progress is being made and facilitate adjustments when deviations are identified.

Attainable/ Achievable

We must determine whether the goals established are attainable, as setting an unachievable goal is futile.

Realistic/Relevant

A goal cannot be achieved if you don't have the tools and skills to achieve it. You can't conduct brain surgery without having training in medicine. We must be realistic in setting our goals.

Time-Bound

A goal is not eternal life and is not supposed to last forever. As such, a deadline must be established for the attainment of the goal. A good goal must be time-bound.

Genie utilised these principles for most of her life decisions, and the evidence speaks for itself, which can be attested to by her multiple academic and professional achievements.

Choosing The Right Team

"Never plan a future with someone that has no future plans for themselves."

—**Author Unknown**

When Genie met Bobby, he seemed quite ambitious as he used to write down his goals and buy and read books so he could enhance his knowledge in Information Technology. Little did Genie know that this was a part of the scam by Bobby and his friend, Paul, to get into her life, pretending that he had goals and was focused.

Genie discovered a few years into her marriage that Bobby was not much of a visionary nor was he the leader he portrayed himself to be in the dating phase of their relationship. He was someone who required leading and, being the man in the relationship, he seemed to have forgotten that he was. Instead of charting the course for his family, Bobby just looked over Genie's shoulder and followed her while she was on her destiny path. When he could not measure up to her, he became jealous and tried to find ways to bring her down to a lower level so he could feel superior.

God created Adam first, then Eve, so the man must be the head of the family, and the wife helps him to achieve the family goals. However, if the man is confused and does not seek guidance from the Lord, what happens then to the family? Eve must take charge. In this instance, Eve was Genie, and when she gave Bobby the ideas to drive the family forward, he became even more resentful and felt inferior. While he was boiling with resentment for his spouse, Genie had to take charge as he was going around in circles like a dog chasing its tail. Bobby was aging, but he was not maturing; he was just a grown aging boy in a man's body.

The Biblical Perspective

In 2 Corinthians 2:17 it states, *"Therefore if any man be in Christ, he is a new creature: old things are passed away; behold, all things are become new."* (KJV). Genie still prayed for Bobby that he would find his way to Jesus and gain some direction for his life. Even though he hurt her, he was still the father of her children, plus the child he had with Delilah Iscariot, as all of them needed him to be at his best to be a good father. She knew he would not listen to her because he felt inferior to her and would take offense from her guidance, so praying was the best she could do. She also forgave him for all he had done to her. She had moved on with her life.

Taking Yourself To A New Dimension

"Success is achieved by the deliberate consistent discipline of taking small steps daily rather than one large step occasionally."
—Mensah Oteh, "The Good Life: Transform Your Life Through One Good Day"

Genie committed herself to learning continually and when she got to Canada, she started attending school to pursue another Master's Degree to gain qualifications in that country and also to make the employment prospects better

67

for herself. She and the children adapted well to the new environment, and she never lost her faith but continued to pray for wisdom like King Solomon. Genie also prayed that she would have her own business again, to leave a legacy for her children and build generational wealth. She knew that she would be successful because the Heavenly Father was her pilot, and she was a lifelong learner and author of her own life story.

"If you don't design your own life plan, chances are you'll fall into someone else's plan. And guess what they have planned for you? Not Much."

—Jim Rohn

Chapter 8

Dear Parents

"Parenting is the easiest thing in the world to have an opinion about but the hardest thing in the world to do."

—Matt Walsh

What Is Parenting?

"When you become a parent, remember: Don't allow anything in your life that you don't want reproduced in your children."

—Mom Quotes - pinterest.com

G enie had empathised with her mother when she became a parent herself and realised that it was a hard job that kept her on her toes 24 hours a day. But she found it quite fulfilling. She understood why her mother resented her, as she saw being a parent as a curse rather than a blessing, as the job was very demanding. Mona-Lisa was not emotionally prepared for the task, as apparently, Genie was an experiment that went wrong. She has not forgiven Genie for coming to earth to this day. Genie, on the other hand, loved parenting, as she got to enhance her negotiating skills, learn incredible patience and was excited about going into the unknown of parenting. It was like "Space, the final frontier." Being chosen to be a parent is a gift from God.

Parenting does not have a job description, but Genie used the Bible as her guide, which was the handbook God gave to humanity to help them raise His children. One of her favourite scripture was Ephesians 6:4 where it states, *"....do not provoke your children to wrath, but bring them up in the training and admonition of the Lord."* (NKJV).

What Is Required For This Job?

Genie's mother, Mona-Lisa, made some miss-steps in her parenting skills but we must bear in mind that she was also just coming out of childhood, and herself lacked parental guidance. Despite the challenges, she tried to be a good parent and was just trying to survive with the child. However, all is not lost as there is hope for parents like Mona-Lisa. According to kidshealth.org, there are nine suggested tips that could help parents to feel more confident and fulfilled in performing their parental duties. These are as follows:

- **Boosting your child's self-esteem** - Praise their accomplishments, be careful with your choice of words and show compassion.

- **Catch children being good** - Compliment them for doing their chores without you asking them and be generous with your affection.

- **Set limits and be consistent with your discipline** - Discipline is important as it teaches children self-control and will result in the behaviour desired by the parent. Being consistent teaches what you expect.

- **Make time for your children** - Children who feel that they aren't seen will act up or misbehave as this is a guaranteed way to get attention. In the previous century, mothers used to be at home nurturing and taking care of their children, but it is now the 21st century, and both parents must work. Don't beat yourself up too much if you don't get to spend as much time as you would like with your children. Make each encounter memorable, and get to know their friends too.

- **Be a good role model** - Display the traits you wish to see in your children, such as respect, friendliness, honesty, kindness, tolerance, and unselfish behavior. Do things for other people without expecting a reward, express thanks, and offer compliments.

71

Above all, treat your children the way you expect other people to treat you.

- **Make communication a priority** - Parents who reason with their kids allow them to understand and learn in a non-judgmental way. Make your expectations clear. If there is a problem, describe it, express your feelings, and invite your child to work on a solution with you.

- **Be flexible and willing to adjust your parenting style** - As your child changes, you will gradually have to change your parenting style. Chances are, what works with your child now will not work in a year or two. Teens tend to look less to their parents and more to their peers for role models, but continue to provide guidance, encouragement, and appropriate discipline, while allowing your teen to earn more independence. Also, seize every opportunity to make a connection.

- **Show that your love is unconditional** - As a parent, you are responsible for correcting and guiding your children. How you express your corrective guidance makes all the difference in how a child receives it. When you must confront your child, avoid blaming, criticizing, or fault-finding, which undermines self-esteem and can lead to resentment. Instead, strive to nurture and encourage, even when disciplining your children. Make sure they know that although you want and expect better next time, your love will not change.

- **Know your own needs and limitation as a parent** – Be honest with yourself and admit that — you are an imperfect parent, and you don't have all the answers. You have strengths and weaknesses as a family leader. Recognize your abilities and, work on your weaknesses, have realistic expectations for yourself, your spouse, and your children. Take time out from parenting to do things that will make you happy as a person (or as a couple). Focusing on your needs does not make you selfish; it simply means you care about your own well-being, which is another important value to model for your children.

Genie did not have a good parental role model to follow in either of her parents, but she took some of the lessons learnt from John Brown, such as ensuring she had a good education among other things, and used them in parenting her children. In the instances where she lacked knowledge, she sought guidance from experienced individuals and her pastor.

As a parent, you owe it to yourself and your children not to stay in your ignorance as there is always someone who has walked this road already and can share their knowledge with you. The work of being a parent will not be easy, but there is a benchmark in the Bible.

An Empowered Parent Moving Forward

Genie did not get frustrated by her parental duties and limitations in her parental skills like her mother did when she used to take out her vengeance on her. She decided that all the trauma she endured would stop with her generation. Her children will not be descendants that are linked to dysfunction, misery, bitterness, and anger. Genie spent years learning and gaining new knowledge and understanding so that she can pass on all she learnt to her children to ensure that she leaves a generation of success, integrity, good character, and nation builders, who mirror the lifestyle of Jesus Christ. She decided that she would use whatever resources available in this new digital information age, such as accessing material online and virtual training sessions to hone her parental skills.

Genie empowered her daughter also to be an independent thinker by ensuring that she is armed with the right information and opportunities to make decisions for herself. She wanted her to be able to analyse situations, make her own decisions and become self-sufficient. From Mona-Lisa's experience, Genie knew the results of being fully dependent on someone else, especially a male that means you no good. She did not want her daughter to get stuck in an abusive relationship with an unwanted pregnancy but to reach her full potential. Genie and Bobby did not have a friendly relationship, but they agreed that they were going to do what was best for the benefit of the children, as the children should not suffer the consequences of adult decisions.

Genie ensured that the children were shown love and taught respect for self and others so that they never felt neglected. She wanted them to be successful, healthy, well-adjusted adults and did everything to protect them from adults or others who meant them no good. Genie knew quite well the side effects of being a neglected child and did not want her children to go searching for love in the wrong places, as they could be led astray by negative influences like gangs or persons who wanted to exploit their innocence.

The Reality Of Life

"When you are getting ready to become a mom, being in love with someone just isn't enough. You need to think about whether he would be a good parent and raise your children with similar beliefs."

—Cindy Crawford

We know that some fathers are pure evil, and if they and the child's mother are not in an intimate relationship, they don't want to support their children unless there is a court order for child support. This is not good parenting or responsible behaviour, as both parents made the decision to have intercourse without protection and were aware of the consequences. There was the possibility that either party could have contracted a sexually transmitted infection (STI) or become a parent, so do the right thing and stand up to your responsibility. Who knows, maybe when you get old, this child might be your chief cornerstone to take care of you in your old age.

William Ross Wallace said that "the hand that rocks the cradle rules the world," meaning that as parents, we have the power within our hands to raise children who will either cause mayhem in society or be positive forces of change that drive humanity forward. Let us look at how our lives would have been if Joseph and Mary were terrible parents to Jesus; who would save us from our sins? Would there be a Joel Osteen if his parents did not create an environment of faith for him to thrive? Look at the impact he is now having around the world.

Parents, you have the power within your hands to change the course of your children's lives. Even if you had a rough start, those struggles will end with your generation. Your children will have a better life than you did, and your generational legacy will be great.

"Parents are the ultimate role models for children. Every word, movement and action has an effect. No other person or outside force has a greater influence on a child than the parent."

—Bob Keeshan

Conclusion

"When life gives you a hundred reasons to cry, show life that you have a thousand reasons to smile."

—UNKNOWN

The Lessons Learnt

Genie's childhood struggles may not be unique to children born to teenage parents, but it is relatable. Being told by your parent constantly that you are a mistake and an unplanned pregnancy and being raised in an environment devoid of love and affection can be a very traumatic experience for a child. This has resulted in many dysfunctional and maladjusted adults like Bobby Chunks.

Genie was very blessed to have found Jesus at an early age and was able to gradually overcome her traumatic past and childhood struggles to become a successful and well-adjusted woman.

Through her hardships, she learnt how to empathise with other persons who were treated as outcasts and was able to master her communication skills and become very conscious of her choice of words when correcting her children. Just

77

like lemons must be squeezed to produce its juice, when Genie was hard-pressed by her husband and the hardships he put her through, she came out like fine gold. She did not crack and lose her mind, but she kept focusing on personal development and achieving the next milestone, and that resulted in her being confident, independent, and a transformational leader.

Genie taught us the benefits of forgiveness and the effects of unforgiveness on one's mental and physical health, and how forgiving others is a powerful tool in helping us to move forward from past hurt and bitterness to achieve our life's purpose.

Forgiveness allows God to give us beauty for ashes, and it has the power to break generational curses in our families. Since we are mere humans, I know that forgiveness is easier said than done, so we must ask Jesus to help us, for those so inclined, or seek the help of a professional to assist with getting over the hurdles. The enemy wanted Genie to be stagnant and spend her life going around in circles, carrying around the burden of shame and past hurt, but she broke the shackles with God's help. She now lives a free, strong, and healthy life.

As individuals, we must never stop learning, whether through formal learning or skills, to keep us energised about life. We must strive to create and seek out opportunities to move our lives and those of others forward through the creation of employment or products that advance humanity. The possibilities are endless when we plan with the Heavenly Father and utilise the SMART method of selecting and actioning our goals.

In charting the course for the future, we must also seek to learn new cultures, travel around our country or internationally to experience a change of environment and widen our frames of reference, form new relationships, and enjoy the fruits of our labour.

Genie changed the path of her generation by encouraging her children emotionally to build their self-esteem, so they could be confident individuals who would create a generation of blessings and a legacy of wealth.

For parents struggling to cope with their personal childhood traumas, there are services available through churches or social programs from the government that can be utilised for support in enhancing your parenting and other life-coping skills.

We may not be born into royalty or a healthy family environment, but we have the power to change and rewrite our life stories because we have a dependable Saviour to help us. He did it for Genie, and He will do it for you.

"Victory comes from finding opportunities in problems."

—Sun Tzu

79

About The Author

Mellisha is an internal auditor by day and a writer by night who has won three bronze medals in the Jamaica Cultural Development Commission (JCDC) Literary Arts competition in 2018 and 2019. She is a graduate of the University of Technology, Jamaica (UTECH), where she attained a Bachelor of Business Administration degree majoring in accounts and a minor in international business. She also holds a certificate in supervisory management with distinction from The University of the West Indies (UWI) Open Campus, among other certifications. Mellisha is the mother of two wonderful children and loves to travel and impart knowledge and encouragement to those she comes in close contact with.

Bibliography

1. Genesis 17 CEV - God's Promise to Abraham - Abram was - Bible Gateway

2. How Generational Curses Affect My Love Life (thesource.org)

3. PURPOSE | definition in the Cambridge English Dictionary

4. Psalm 139 NIV - For the director of music. Of David. A - Bible Gateway

5. www.smart-goals-guide.com/smart-goal-setting.html

6. Nine Steps to More Effective Parenting (for Parents) - Nemours KidsHealth

7. Goal Definition & Meaning - Merriam-Webster

* 9 7 8 1 9 5 3 7 5 9 9 4 8 *